KU-453-201

Schools Library and Information Services

S00000652518

Travel Through Time
War Machines

Military Vehicles Past and Present

Jane Shuter

www.raintreepublishers.co.uk
Visit our website to find out more information about **Raintree** books.

To order:
☎ Phone 44 (0) 1865 888112
▤ Send a fax to 44 (0) 1865 314091
▥ Visit the Raintree Bookshop at **www.raintreepublishers.co.uk** to browse our catalogue and order online.

First published in Great Britain by Raintree, Halley Court, Jordan Hill, Oxford OX2 8EJ, part of Harcourt Education.
Raintree is a registered trademark of Harcourt Education Ltd.

© Harcourt Education Ltd 2004
The moral right of the proprietor has been asserted.

All rights reserved. No part of this publication may be reproduced, stored in a retrieval system, or transmitted in any form or by any means, electronic, mechanical, photocopying, recording, or otherwise, without either the prior written permission of the publishers or a licence permitting restricted copying in the United Kingdom issued by the Copyright Licensing Agency Ltd, 90 Tottenham Court Road, London W1T 4LP (www.cla.co.uk).

Editorial: Nick Hunter and Catherine Clarke
Design: Michelle Lisseter and bigtop
Picture Research: Maria Joannou and Kathryn Kollberg
Production: Jonathan Smith

Originated by Dot Gradations Ltd
Printed and bound in China by South China Printing Company

ISBN 1 844 43507 5
08 07 06 05 04
10 9 8 7 6 5 4 3 2 1

British Library Cataloguing in Publication Data
Shuter, Jane
War Machines: military vehicles past and present – (Travel Through Time)
358.2'5'09
A full catalogue record for this book is available from the British Library.

Acknowledgements
The publishers would like to thank the following for permission to reproduce photographs:
Ancient Art and Architecture Collection p. **8**; ATM Images p. **15**, Corbis pp. **25**, **29**; Defence Picture Library pp. **5**, **17**, **21**, **27**, **28**; Harcourt Education p. **18**; Hulton Archive pp. **16**, **20**, **22**, **23**, **24**, **26**; Michael Holford pp. **6**, **7**; National Maritime Museum Greenwich p. **12**; Peter Newark's Military Photos pp. **9**, **10**, **11**, **14**, **19**; Robert Harding Picture Library p. **7**; Topham Picturepoint p. **13**; Werner Forman p. **4**.

Cover photograph of an image of World War II reproduced with permission of Art Archive.

Every effort has been made to contact copyright holders of any material reproduced in this book. Any omissions will be rectified in subsequent printings if notice is given to the publishers.

The paper used to print this book comes from sustainable resources.

BROMLEY PUBLIC LIBRARIES

L -47439

652518   SCH

J 358.2

Contents

Any words appearing in bold, **like this**, are explained in the Glossary.

Fighting machines

Different groups of people have fought each other since the earliest times. Being able to move further and faster than the enemy makes an army more likely to win. **Chariots** were first used in battle over 4000 years ago. Since then, armies have tried to **invent** faster and more deadly vehicles.

In ancient times, soldiers rode horses into battle, sometimes firing arrows at the enemy.

Soldiers wear **armour,** which covers their bodies with a hard surface. This makes it harder to injure them. Vehicles are also covered in armour. Too much armour makes a vehicle slow and difficult to drive. Vehicles and people need enough armour to be safe, but not so much that they cannot move around easily.

There is no one on board this unmanned military vehicle (UVA). The **pilot** 'flies' it from a safe place.

SAFEST OF ALL

Early armies fought hand-to-hand. By the early 1900s people could fight from vehicles that protected them. Modern armies often fight from a distance. Powerful **weapons** can be fired many hundreds of kilometres by a soldier who is safe in a hidden control room.

War chariots

The first military vehicles were **Sumerian** war chariots, pulled by horses. The Sumerians are the first people we know of that used the wheel. They used their chariots to carry equipment, as well as in battle. Without air-filled tyres to protect them, the road surface would have been bumpy!

This Sumerian box was made in about 2500 BC. It shows their war chariots.

Safer than on foot?

As time passed, people wanted to make war chariots faster and easier to turn and move. The best way to do this was to make the chariot smaller and lighter. They cut down the sides of the chariot, and used wheels that were not solid.

EGYPTIAN CHARIOTS

Ancient Egyptian war chariots were very light. This made them fast, but the driver had to be good at controlling the chariot and horses. The chariots easily overturned if they hit a rock.

This box shows the pharaoh Tutankhamen in his war chariot, fighting his enemies.

Early warships

Early warships were built to move fast, to **ram** and to sink enemy ships. The earliest descriptions of sea battles are from the ancient Greeks. They talk of the sounds of splintering wood and screaming as ships rammed into each other and jammed together.

GREEK WARSHIPS

Greek warships had a heavy ram at the front of the ship. They were about 3.6 metres wide and 36 metres long. About 170 rowers were packed close together on three levels. These ships had no sails. Later warships had sails that they took down when they went into battle.

This is a modern model of an ancient Greek warship. When they overturned, very few rowers escaped.

8

Capture!

From about 1200 BC warships were bigger, heavier and powered by oars and sails. They cost a lot and took a long time to build. So sailors tried to board and capture enemy ships, not sink them. These warships, called **galleys,** would still rather ram and sink the enemy than lose the battle. These ships had fewer rowers than early warships. They carried more soldiers, including **archers** who fired arrows at the enemy from far away.

The Chinese were the first people to use **rudders** to steer their ships.

Cannon at sea

The Chinese used **gunpowder** from about AD 1000, mainly in huge firework displays. It was not used much in sea battles until **cannon** were **invented** in about AD 1300. Cannon fired heavy iron cannonballs, which could easily make holes in the sides of a ship and sink it. Once cannon were invented, warships had to change.

The Battle of Lepanto in 1571 was the last big battle where galleys were used.

At first, cannon were just put on the decks of **galley** ships. Because of their weight, the cannon made ships harder to move. They also bounced back after firing cannonballs, which could overturn the ship.

BOSTON

CHARLES TOWN

This painting shows British ships attacking Bunker Hill, Boston, USA, in 1775, during the War of American Independence.

A new design

The first warship built to carry cannon, the English *Mary Rose*, built between 1509 and 1510, had cannon on deck and below deck. This made the ship very heavy and hard to move around. By 1600, ships had more sails to use the wind to move faster and to change direction more easily. Ships armed with cannon attacked land as well as other ships at sea.

Life on a man-of-war

In the 1700s and 1800s fighting ships developed. There were several different sizes of ships. The biggest, a **first rate** man-of-war, could carry over 100 **cannon** and nearly 900 sailors. Life on board was hard for the sailors, even when they were not fighting battles.

This painting from the 1800s of life below decks shows things as far cleaner and less crowded than they really were.

OFFICERS AND MEN

The captain had his own **cabin** and dining room. The officers in charge of the ship shared a small room with bunks. The ordinary sailors slept in hammocks slung up over the cannon on the gun decks. They had no privacy at all.

Sailors got up at dawn, scrubbing the decks and cleaning the ship until 6 a.m. They had porridge for breakfast, and 'Scotch coffee', a drink made from burnt oatmeal and hot water. At midday they had salted meat, dried peas, soaked and boiled, and ships biscuits. These biscuits were made from flour and water with a pinch of salt, and were baked hard. For some sailors, the last meal of the day was porridge.

After a tough battle, sailors might gather together to pray for their wounded.

Submarines

Submarines are underwater warships that can creep up on the enemy without being seen. The first submarine was the *Hunley*, built in 1863 during the American Civil War. It moved just under the surface of the water, driven by eight men turning a pole joined to the **propeller**. The *Hunley* sank an enemy ship, the *Housatonic*, by **ramming** it under water with a **torpedo**. Unfortunately the *Hunley* also sank, maybe because the explosion churned the water and turned it over.

This is a painting of the *Hunley* submarine. Once the sailors were inside they had no air and no light except a candle.

Modern submarines, such as this one, have large crews and lots of equipment.

NUCLEAR SUBMARINES

Nuclear submarines can stay under water for months – longer than other submarines. They do not need to come up every few hours or days to get air as some others do.

Staying under

Submarines were used in
World War I (1914–18) and
World War II (1939–45). They were stronger and
bigger than earlier submarines and could dive further
and stay under water longer. The *Hunley* could stay
under water for 25 minutes. By 1940 submarines
stayed under for several hours or days. They fired
torpedoes over longer distances. They had periscopes
to look above the water, without coming up.

All at sea

By 1900 fighting ships were made of metal and were bigger and heavier than men-of-war. They were not powered by rowing or using sails to catch the wind, but by steam engines. These battleships were much bigger and had more **weapons**. They, and their weapons, were expensive to make. If the enemy sank a battleship, it cost a lot to replace.

DESTROYERS

Destroyers were small, fast ships that travelled with large battleships, to keep them safe. They carried **torpedoes** to attack enemy ships before they could get close enough to fire on the battleships.

Destroyers also had to defend battleships against submarines.

As ships got bigger they had to stay further away from the shore. Soldiers had to use landing craft like these to get to land.

In 1914 World War I began. Both sides began to change ships ready for war. From about 1910, long, flat decks were made on some ships, so planes could take off and land on them. These ships, called aircraft carriers, were not used in battle until close to the end of the war, in 1918. When **submarines** began to sink ships, **sonar** was developed. Sonar bounced sound waves off large objects under water so submarines could be found and sunk.

Transport

All armies wanted fighting machines, but they also needed more ordinary military vehicles. They needed to move their soldiers and equipment around quickly. They also needed vehicles to get the wounded soldiers off the battlefield and into hospital.

In the 1200s roads were so bad that it was easier for soldiers to move heavy supplies by sea.

Quick march

In earliest times armies used animals such as horses, oxen and camels to carry their supplies or pull carts full of supplies. The army leaders rode horses, but ordinary soldiers had to march.

As trucks, ships and planes were **invented**, they were used to transport soldiers and their equipment. Sometimes special types of transport were **designed** for armies. One example is the aircraft carrier, a ship with a special runway for planes to take off and land.

JEEPS

Jeeps were first made for the US army around 1940. They were called General Purpose Vehicles (GP for short). This became 'jeep'. Jeeps were small and quite light. They could easily speed across very bumpy ground.

This World War II jeep has just hit a very big bump!

Tanks

Tanks were big vehicles covered with **armour**, with a big gun on the top. Tanks were first used in World War I. They were very heavy, but had 'tracks' to spread the weight and carry them over bumpy ground. The first time they were used in battle was by the British in 1916.

RIDING IN A TANK

Riding in a 1916 tank was hot and airless. The crew inside could only see out of the few air slits and holes for the **weapons**. The crew were thrown around inside the tank as it travelled over bumpy ground.

This early US tank was photographed in 1917.

Better designs

Tanks have been used ever since 1916. Their **design** has been changed to make the ride less bumpy and to help the crew see more. Modern tanks also have radios to keep in touch with their base. Their armour plating keeps the crew safe from bullets. If they are hit by more powerful **ammunition**, such as bombs dropped from aircraft, it is hard for the crew to get out before the fuel tank explodes.

These modern tanks have been designed to fight in hot, sandy deserts.

Early fighter planes

The first **fighter planes** flew during World War I. There were big planes, with a crew of up to eight, and planes for just one **pilot**. There were planes made of **canvas** and wood and others made of metal. Some planes had two wings on each side, others just one. All sorts of planes were open to the air, so the pilots and crew got very cold.

The Wright Brothers, who invented the aeroplane, made this first fighter plane for the US army.

What were they used for?

Planes were first used for photographing enemy bases. Then pilots dropped bombs on the enemy. Pilots dropped the first bombs by hand, one by one. At first, pilots fought each other with handguns, then with guns fixed to the planes.

This photograph of Baron von Richthofen was taken in 1916.

THE RED BARON

One of the most famous fighter pilots of World War I was Baron von Richthofen, who shot down 80 British planes. He was nicknamed 'The Red Baron' because he had his plane painted bright red. He was shot down on 21 April 1918.

Battles in the skies

Planes played a big part in World War II. There were two sorts of planes: **fighters** and **bombers**. Fighter planes were small and light, with just the **pilot** on board. They flew at around 596 kilometres (370 miles) per hour. Fighters only had enough fuel to fly about 757 kilometres (470 miles). Bomber planes, with a crew of five and heavy bombs on board, were bigger, heavier and slower. They flew at around 354 kilometres (220 miles) per hour at best. They could fly about 2400 kilometres (1500 miles), though.

This B17 bomber plane was photographed in 1945.

Both sides bombed each other's cities and also soldiers, airbases and ships. It was an air attack on the US fleet at Pearl Harbor, Hawaii, by the Japanese that pulled the USA into the war.

AIR INVENTIONS

New inventions could take time to be used, after they were first invented. They had to be tested for safety, and people trained to use them properly.

what?	why?	first used
radar	to spot aircraft using radio waves	1936
jet engines	to go faster	1939
helicopters	to land in difficult places	1939

This photograph shows Japanese planes coming in to attack Pearl Harbor in 1941.

Planes since 1945

Since 1945 fighting planes have changed a great deal. New technology has made them lighter, stronger and faster. It has also made them more expensive. A World War II **bomber** would cost around US$200,000 to build today. A modern bomber plane costs hundreds of millions of US dollars to build.

HELICOPTERS

Helicopters have a large rotor blade on the top that spins round very fast to make them fly. They are useful in wars because they do not need a lot of space to take off and land. They have problems, too. They cannot carry much weight. They do not have a lot of space inside and they are very noisy.

These helicopters have just dropped US soldiers off in a jungle clearing.

The 'stealth bomber' has a special coating on the outside, which makes it hard for enemy radar to spot.

Modern fighting planes have a lot of complicated equipment. Computer technology tracks other planes, works out where the **pilots** are and can even be set to fire **weapons** for them. The US army is very close to having a working plane that can be flown almost anywhere in the world by a pilot back in the USA.

Modern wars

Armies that can use the latest modern technology do not need to travel to fight. They can fire **missiles** over long distances to drop bombs that cause huge damage to the enemy. They can strike at once, rather than having to transport soldiers and machines to another place to fight.

This is a US Multiple Launched Rocket System (MLRS).

Computerized wars

Ships and other military vehicles are now worked by fewer people. Computers do much of the work that people once did. Scientists think that it will soon be possible to drive almost any vehicle by computer.

Wars are usually about taking over another country. Even if they begin fighting at a distance, by computer, soldiers have to go to the country they are taking over at some point. They have to go there to keep control. Then they will need ordinary military vehicles.

NOT ALL MODERN

Wars in developing countries, especially smaller wars inside a country or wars fought by small armies from hiding, do not have expensive, modern equipment. These armies still use older military equipment, including vehicles.

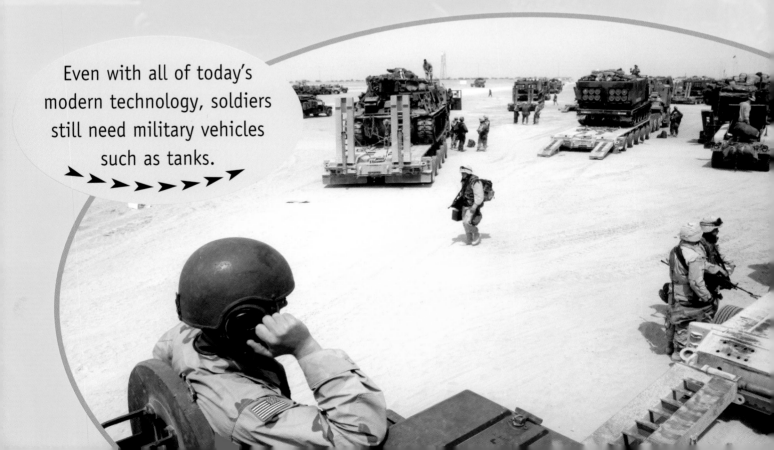

Even with all of today's modern technology, soldiers still need military vehicles such as tanks.

Find out for yourself

You can find out more about the history of military vehicles by talking to older people about how these vehicles have changed during their lifetimes. Your local library will have books about this. They may have newspapers and magazine articles, as well. You will find the answers to many of your questions in this book, but you can also use other books and the Internet.

Books to read

Designed For Success: Attack Fighters, Ian Graham (Heinemann Library, 2003)

Take off!: Transport around the world: Planes, Chris Oxlade (Heinemann Library, 2001)

Using the Internet

Explore the Internet to find out more about military vehicles. Websites can change, but if the link below no longer works, don't worry. Use a search engine, such as www.yahooligans.com or www.internet4kids.com, and type in keywords such as **'tank'**, **'fighter plane'**, **'submarine'** and 'jeep'.

Websites

http://www.bbc.co.uk/schools/vikings/travel/index.shtml
Find out more about Viking ships and warriors.

Disclaimer
All the Internet addresses (URLs) given in this book were valid at the time of going to press. However, due to the dynamic nature of the Internet, some addresses may have changed, or sites may have ceased to exist since publication. While the author and publishers regret any inconvenience this may cause readers, no responsibility for any such changes can be accepted by either the author or the publishers.

Glossary

ammunition anything that is fired at the enemy to harm them

archer soldier who fires arrows from a bow

armour something that is used to protect soldiers or machines

bomber aircraft made to drop bombs

cabin room inside a vehicle

cannon large, heavy gun on wheels that fires large iron balls using gunpowder

canvas strong fabric

chariot platform on wheels, pulled by a horse or horses

design to plan, or decide how to make something

fighter plane aircraft made to fight with other aircraft

first rate ships were given a rating depending on their size. First rate were the biggest.

galley long, narrow ship powered by oars and sometimes sails, too

gunpowder mixture of chemical powders that explodes when lit

invent to make or discover something for the first time

missile anything that is thrown to hurt someone. Modern missiles have bombs fixed to them.

pilot person who flies a plane

propeller blade-shaped part of a ship or aeroplane that turns to make it move

ram to hit hard at speed

rudder oar at the back of a ship that moves to change the direction of the ship

sonar when sound waves are bounced off large objects to locate them

submarine underwater ship

Sumerian person or object coming from the ancient country of Sumer, which is now southern Iraq

tank big vehicle covered with armour, with a big gun on the top

torpedo weapon fired from a distance under water

weapon object used for fighting

Index

Titles in the *Travel Through Time* series include:

Hardback   1 844 43506 7

Hardback   1 844 43502 4

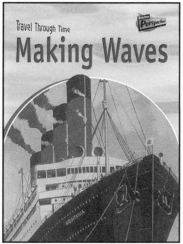

Hardback   1 844 43503 2

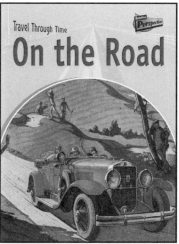

Hardback   1 844 43504 0

Hardback   1 844 43505 9

Hardback   1 844 43507 5

Find out about the other titles in this series on our website www.raintreepublishers.co.uk